Dr. Lynn Marie Morski is a physician, attorney, and lifelong quitting enthusiast. She practices medicine at the Veterans Administration and shares her love of strategic quitting through speaking, coaching, and her podcast, *Quit Happens*. Her goal is to pass on the strategic quitting skills she's developed to help people go from settling to succeeding. When she's not doctoring, lawyering, or evangelizing quitting, Dr. Morski is also a certified yoga instructor, trains the Brazilian martial art of capoeira, plays guitar and bass, and dances like everyone is watching.

Dedication

For my parents, who supported each and every one of my quits.

Hey Susan,
Thank you so
much for coming to
the lunch & learn!
Best of luck with your Quits!,

QUITTING BY DESIGN

Learn to Use Strategic Quitting
as a Tool to Carve out a Successful Life

Dr. Lynn Marie Morski

AUSTIN MACAULEY PUBLISHERS™
LONDON • CAMBRIDGE • NEW YORK • SHARJAH

Ordering Information:
Quantity sales: special discounts are available on quantity purchases by corporations, associations, and others. For details, contact the publisher at the address below.

Publisher's Cataloging-in-Publication data
Morski Dr. Lynn Marie.
Quitting By Design

ISBN 9781641825368.(Paperback)
ISBN 9781641825375.(Hardback)
ISBN 9781641825382.(E-Book)

The main category of the book —. Self-help & personal development

www.austinmacauley.com

First Published (2018)
Austin Macauley Publishers ™
40 Wall Street, 28th Floor
New York, NY 10005
USA

mail-usa@austinmacauley.com
+1 (646) 5125767

Acknowledgments

My deepest gratitude goes out to everyone who supported my pre-sale by buying a copy (or several) of the book: John Lin, Chad Peace, Fred von Graf, Thomas Jarboe, Frank Morski, Adrienne Stewart, Alex Corrales, Alex Vences, Alex Gauthier, Alvaro Perez, Amy Porter, Massape, Andrew Bianchi, Angie Hanchett, Anthony Astolfi, Apoorva Mallya, Arash Afshar, Arthur Wentworth, Autumn Houston, Benjamin Butron, Beverly Tuazon, Carla Ruiz-Velasco, Carlos Armijo, Christine Mersand, David Biglari and Ciara Bozarth, Dennis Stein, Deon Pearson, Don Hutcheson, Donna Kloustermeyer, Eric Dean, Erica Siegal, Geoff Abram, Heemesh Seth, Jackie Silber, James Dutton, Jamie Zaffino, Jeremy Castellano, Jessica Vazquez, Jim Jonas, Jissa Valerio-Woss, Jonathan Kalman, Jordan Woerndle, Josemar Castillo, Joshua Stewart, Judy Bugger, Karen Kuhl, Kathy Lomaskin, Kathy Davis, Katie Allen (O'Donnell – for you KT), Kevin Hwang, Kimmie D'Amico, Lee Constantine, Lester Ancheta, Levani Korganashvili, Marjan Rashedi, Maulik Shah and Sarjita Shukla, Meredith and Brother Morski, Nemo Curiel, Nicole Barrote, Nidhi Kukreja, Patricia Castro, Patakiss Hall, Paul Hanna, Pete Dewar, Ram Kumar, Ramon Gonzalez, Rea Young, Ricardo Booth, Sasha Korbut, Satkirin Khalsa, Sean Jones, Sharmila Hall, Shawn Griffiths, Sheila Cope, Shelly Stewart, Siddique Abbasi, Skye Giordano, Tina Mahajan, and Tracey Minutolo. Your support in my time of anxiety-producing, shameless self-promotion kept me going and I am endlessly grateful for the encouragement.

The rest of the acknowledgements will be in order along my quitting journey…

To Pop, who always thought I'd be a doctor or a lawyer, but who still supported all those other things I tried to be.

To Mom, who (aside from the eyebrow tattoos) has never questioned a single decision I ever made. That kind of freedom is invaluable.

To Tracey Minutolo, for sending my quitting speech to Scott Bartlow from Happen to Your Career, which led to my first podcast interview about quitting…and for your endless invaluable side-hustle coaching and help with promotion. You are a true gem.

To Arash Afshar, for showing me how to set up a podcast and for always supporting my artistic and self-improvement endeavors.

To Tom Jarboe, for showing up out of nowhere to help me campaign to be a Bernie delegate, which set off a cascade of awesomeness for which I can never thank you enough.

To Chad Peace, for believing in a Bernie crier socialist Russian spy. You gave me opportunities beyond anything I could have ever fathomed. I told myself after the DNC I wanted to focus on election reform and suddenly there you were, handing me the keys. You opened up an entire new world to me, and I am eternally grateful for your confidence and support.

To Kyle Haller, for the killer cover design, and to everyone at IVC Media, for showing me how to do social media marketing, then showing me again when I'd inevitably forget.

To Lee Constantine and Publishizer, for giving me a platform through which to pre-sell my book, and for being beyond helpful during the pre-sale.

And finally to David Shyde, for meeting with me at a coffee shop to help figure out what I was supposed to do with my life. Out of that meeting came the *Quitting by Design* website, which would have never happened without your design/photography expertise and your encouragement. Every step of the way you've given me the perfect advice, exactly when I needed it, both personally and professionally. Obrigada, DVG…sua amizade é tão importante para mim. Nunca esquecerei tudo o que você me deu. ~ Ms. Power.

Introduction

At some point we decide what we want to be when we grow up. At another point we decide where we want to live. At yet another point we decide with whom we want to spend our lives.

Are you currently in the first career, locale, or relationship you chose? Me neither.

And that's ok. Actually, that's great. Because life is about growing and learning every single day, and about being more in tune with yourself and your desires today than you were yesterday. We were not given this one life just to settle for less than ideal situations.

Realize that any decision you made prior to today was made by a person different from who you are now; one with less knowledge than you currently possess: less knowledge about you and others, and society as a whole. And if your former self made a decision that no longer works for you, there's great news:

You can quit.

In fact, you probably should quit. And you don't have to do it alone. This book is for anyone who has a job, a career, a relationship, a living situation, an educational pursuit, a mindset, an ANYTHING that may not be working well.

Quitting isn't a dirty word. Settling is. A good friend of mine refers to settling as 'suicide of the soul,' and I couldn't agree more.

Let's do this. Together. Let's start quitting.

Chapter 1

A Word About Semantics

I'm well aware that many people cringe when they hear the word 'quit,' and even more cringe at the thought of being called a quitter. A friend of mine summed it up best when he said, "We've all lost things in life, yet none of us wants to be called a loser. That's the struggle I have with the word 'quitter.' " And I get that. Technically one who quits is a quitter. But that's just semantics. And I think his example of the term 'loser' actually works well. We have all lost something—even if it's just a game of chess or arm wrestling. Do we then walk around for the rest of our lives self-identifying as losers? I should hope not! Similarly, having quit something at some point in our lives shouldn't define us as quitters.

Here's another way of thinking about the semantics involved. Imagine all the online gurus whose aim is to help you lead your best life. They often suggest making positive changes—and there are two forms that change can take: adding something or subtracting something. For you to change jobs, you have to subtract your old job and add a new one. What's another way of referring to that subtraction? Quitting. Another way to rephrase the ever-popular 'I'm in transition…' is to say, 'I quit something, and I am about to do something else.' There are a thousand ways to refer to making a change for the better, but most of them involve removing things that weren't working – also known as quitting.

If you think about it, 'quitter' is a label we only ascribe to people whose quit we don't support. For example, imagine you are working in a fast-food restaurant waiting for your big break in Hollywood, and then you get that break and start making enough money that you no longer need to work in fast food. Does anyone call you a quitter when you quit slinging burgers? Never! They'd say "You made it." Yet you definitely quit something, and, ergo, are a quitter.

If despite the above examples, the word 'quitting' still makes you uneasy or brings up negative feelings, feel free to replace it with 'changing' or 'redefining' or 'transitioning.' Because the name isn't important— what's important is that you find your way out of whatever isn't serving you and into something that will.

Chapter 2

Should I Quit Something?

Many of us think quitting is something that only applies to a job or smoking, but quitting can apply to every area of your life. For example, you can quit something as insignificant as a gym membership, or something with a significantly larger effect on your life, like a relationship or marriage. You can quit things that are bad for you and you can quit things that are seemingly good for you. Take that gym membership. Is working out generally good for your health? Absolutely. But does quitting your gym membership mean you've given up on working out? Absolutely not! You may have found that running trails outside or taking a martial arts class is more your speed. You may have found a group that does free CrossFit exercises in the park. You're not quitting working out. You're quitting one means of working out that isn't working out for you any longer.

Now that hopefully I've taken a bit of the stigma off quitting, let's get back to the original question: Is there something you need to quit? Here's a good place to start investigating. Is there a certain time of day, email subject line, caller ID name, or personal interaction that you can 'feel' in your stomach? What do I mean by this? Imagine the sensations in your body when you see flashing police lights in your rearview mirror. If you're anything like me, your stomach probably sinks. In my experience, the first sign that something in my life may need to be on the chopping block is that I can feel my stomach drop when I have to deal with it.

When I was co-founder of a startup, the sound of my work email going off always resulted in an instant feeling of dread. One day it hit me: if I'm going about my day, perfectly happy, and a single sound can result in a 180-degree change in my mood, maybe I should make a 180-degree change in my job.

Or maybe it's not a sinking feeling in your stomach, but it's some other method your body has decided to use as your wake-up call. In my experience as a doctor, the body's two favorite wake-up calls are digestive issues and insomnia. Stress can trigger acid reflux, and it can cause or worsen the cramping and diarrhea of irritable bowel syndrome.

This connection between your thoughts and your gastrointestinal system is not imaginary. There's a true, scientific basis to it. Inside your GI tract is something called the enteric nervous system (ENS) which consists of over 100 million nerve cells, running from esophagus to rectum. Thoughts that originate in your brain translate into signals your brain sends to the ENS which lead to responses such as moving food more quickly or slowly through the digestive system.

Similarly, anxiety, depression, and stress can all keep you awake at night or wake you up in the middle of the night. If you're one of the way too many people who suffer from sleep-onset insomnia (the inability to fall asleep at night), I ask you to examine what you're thinking about as you lie awake. Are you having a rough time sleeping because you're dreading waking up and going to work? Or is it because you're still ruminating over an argument you had with your spouse over dinner? These can be great clues in determining what may not be working.

What does this look like for you? I truly hope that there's nothing in your life that results in your stress level spiking, your stomach sinking, your acid refluxing or your sleep not happening, but if there is, I highly recommend starting to investigate that feeling. Many people refer to those internal feelings as your intuition. Is your intuition telling you there's an issue? Can you change the situation? Do you need to quit the endeavor or relationship that disrupts your happiness? If so, don't worry. I won't leave you hanging here to quit on your own. In the next section we'll cover more specifics on what exactly to quit, and in subsequent chapters, we'll cover what keeps people from quitting, the difference between quitting and failing, some of the moral value we've attached to quitting, and other related topics that will help you make the decisions that will lead to your best life.

Before we go forward, I want to mention that in some situations you may benefit from quits that don't lead to the above symptoms. I was speaking with someone who was thinking about leaving his relationship. I told him that I knew social media can be misleading, but from what I saw on Facebook it looked like his relationship was a pretty happy one. He told me that my perceptions were accurate. There wasn't any fighting or anything particularly unpleasant about his relationship. So why was he contemplating leaving? Because he had goals—and his partner did not necessarily share or understand those goals, which is a completely valid reason to explore quitting a relationship.

There's a work equivalent to this scenario as well. A friend of mine had a great job he enjoyed, but he felt a calling to start working full-time in storytelling. He eventually quit the full-time job—the one that wasn't giving him any particular anxiety or insomnia or stress—so that he could pursue his dreams. There are plenty of situations which may be comfortable for us, but we should beware of those that make us, as the song says, *comfortably numb*. Numb isn't a great state of mind for forward progress.

I throw these examples in here to let you know that just because you're sleeping well and your gut isn't telling you anything is wrong, it's still a good idea to make sure everything you're involved with is going to provide you with the best chance at achieving your goals, whatever they may be. Evaluate whether you might want to quit your good job in pursuit of a better one, leave your comfortable city and move to one with even bigger opportunities, and separate from a relationship that's pleasant but not inspiring or supportive of your dreams.

And finally, if you've gotten this far, done a thorough examination of your current situation, and decided nothing is in need of a quit, then congratulations! But I'd suggest you not put down the book just yet, as strategic quitting is an important self-care tool and life skill that will undoubtedly benefit you at some time in the future, even if it's just knowing how to decide NOT to quit something. If nothing else, developing the practice of listening to your body is worth its weight in gold for both your physical and mental health. If you suffer from chronic headaches, they could be due to stress, or they could be signs of a serious physical medical condition. Either way, if you don't notice and pay attention to symptoms like this, you can't address them, and they can turn from smaller issues into more lasting concerns.

Chapter 3

What Keeps People from Quitting?

If you've listened to your intuition and discovered an area of your life that could benefit from a quit, there may now be something else nagging at you. The 'what-ifs.'

If you don't immediately know what the 'what-ifs' are, then congratulations, you may be a professional-level quitter. But for most, the thought of quitting leads to an initial wave of relief that is often followed by the following thoughts:

- What if I never find another job or relationship?
- What if everyone thinks less of me because I quit?
- What if this was the best option I had?
- What if I fail at my new endeavor?

I was listening to a podcast called 'Tangentially Speaking' in which a 57-year-old psychiatrist spoke about how she recently quit traditional medicine and was embarking on a career in more holistic medicine. The woman was a multi-lingual, respected doctor who had worked in war zones in Africa delivering babies at some point in her career, and yet she very bluntly said, "I'm afraid." The podcast host, a psychologist himself, pointed out that "any transition creates fear because you're going to the unknown, and what scares you is that you can't see it." He called it the psychic equivalent of jumping into a cold lake. So if you're afraid and feeling alone, know that it's totally natural, as we're biologically ingrained to fear the unknown, to fear what lies on the other side of that quit.

I was right there with you and I still experience a lower level of these fears every time I face another quit. Remember, I may be a professional quitter now (yes, I'm officially making that a thing), but 20 years ago quitting was much harder and I recall very well being caught in a swirl of these same fears. A lot of the quits I made required me to leave my comfort zone (like having a steady job), and leap into the uncomfortable unknown (like applying to medical school.)

There's a quote from the book, *You Are a Badass at Making Money* that always amused me. The book's author, Jen Sincero, says the following, "The walls of your comfort zone are lovingly decorated with your lifelong collection of favorite excuses." And lest you think you are alone, you should take a look inside my comfort zone. It's like the *Crate and Barrel* of excuses. But I bet if you look at what's behind your excuses (let's be slightly gentler and call them 'reasons not to leave the zone'), you'll probably find good ol' fear hanging out.

In the next few sections we'll dissect some of the fears you may have. But let's acknowledge the basic truth: quitting isn't easy. It involves risk and action. It involves change, which in and of itself can be scary, no matter what the change is.

Before we move on, remember that if you're plagued with doubts and fears, it's completely normal. Being hard on yourself for having these feelings is not going to help give you the clarity you need to address the tough questions, so just breathe easy and know that while your fears are valid, you aren't the first person to quit, nor will you be the last. Almost everyone in your shoes has had the same thoughts. They've still succeeded, and you can too.

Chapter 4

What About All That Time and Money I Wasted?

It's time for one of my favorite topics involved in quitting: wasted time and money. Imagine you are thinking of leaving a relationship you've been in for five years. It's not going very well and it doesn't bring you any of the joy it once did. But when you think of leaving, your first thought is, "If I leave, I've wasted five years…"

Or say you've worked at a company for ten years. You're miserable and there's no obvious end in sight to whatever is bothering you about the job, but you stay, because leaving means you would have 'wasted' those ten years.

These periods of time spent in an endeavor are what economists refer to as 'sunk costs.' They are in the past and you can't get them back, no matter what you do in the future. The 'sunk cost fallacy' refers to the fact that people are often hesitant to quit something that they've already invested a lot of time or money in, so they'll continue to sink more time and more money into it.

Let me show you the sunk cost fallacy in action. You go to eat at an expensive restaurant, and halfway through your dinner, you are uncomfortably full. You have a decision to make: stop eating or finish the meal. Does finishing the meal get you your money back? NO. You're financially in the same position you would be had you just stopped eating.

You gained nothing but a stomachache and an additional hour at the gym.

If you can see where the rationale behind finishing the meal is flawed, try to apply that to your current situation. I had to do just that when I decided to quit pursuing my master's degree in multimedia. The program was two years long, and I had already paid for and completed the first year by the time I realized I never wanted to do multimedia in the future. At that point I had a decision to make—spend another year and another few thousand dollars to get the degree, or cut my losses, quit, and begin pursuing something more in line with my new goals.

Let's get back to that five-year relationship I referenced above. Let's also assume, for sake of argument, that most relationships have the end goal of marriage. Therefore, dating is essentially a process of finding someone with whom you would want to spend the rest of your life. Most pre-marriage relationships are generally the period of time where you test out whether a person is someone with whom you feel you would be compatible in the long-term.

With all those assumptions in place, I ask you to revisit the scenario. You've been in a relationship for five years, and you're contemplating leaving it, presumably because it's not working for reasons that you've determined are not remediable. Why would you want to continue on toward spending the rest of your life with someone who isn't working for you now? Marriage isn't easy, so heading into it with someone you already feel incompatible with sounds like a recipe for disaster in most circumstances.

And the same goes for many jobs. Having dedicated five years to a company whose culture doesn't work for you at all is no reason to keep dedicating more years to it. What would the goal be there? To climb the career ladder in a company you don't like? To have a job that requires you to spend more time in the culture you find toxic?

At this point I'll insert my periodic reminder that you get ONE life. Ok, for the reincarnation fans out there, I'll clarify: *this you* gets *this one* life. Why spend more of it in a situation that makes you unhappy, unfulfilled, and unsatisfied?

ONE LIFE.

So please, dump the sunk costs fallacy and make sure the rest of the time and money you spend is spent on something that leads to increased happiness, not continued stress. You deserve it.

Chapter 5

What Are You Missing Out on If You Don't Quit?

With this one life we have, there is a finite number of things we can do. In fact, at any one time there's really only one thing we can be doing. Now you're going to say, "But I can talk on the phone and cook at the same time!" Sure, for many daily duties we can try to multitask. But for a lot of larger issues, that's not the case. You can only have one 40-hour a week, 9 to 5 job, because you can't spend those 40 hours, between 9 and 5, at two places. You can only be enrolled in one graduate school program at a time. And unless you're into polyamory, you can only be in one relationship at a time.

This brings us to another economic concept that deals directly with the above. It's called 'opportunity costs' and it refers to the cost of what you are missing out on if you stay in your current situation. For example, if you stay in an unsatisfying relationship, you're missing out on the opportunity to be in a better relationship. And if you stay in a job that's not right for you, you are missing out on the opportunity to find one that is.

Now you may be currently looking for a better job while staying in one you don't like, but you plan to quit once you find a new opportunity. That's fine. But this concept applies most directly to relationships. You can't wholeheartedly be looking for another relationship while you're currently in one. Or more appropriately, you shouldn't be. If you are, then you need to quit that relationship now to be fair to your partner. A relationship is not like a job. Where you may need to hang on to a job while looking for a new one in order to pay rent, you do not need to hang onto a relationship. In fact you shouldn't (and I'm not a big fan of imposing my values on you, but here's the one time I'm going to 'should' all over you!). You should quit whatever relationship isn't fulfilling to you, so you can begin the emotional separation process that will lead to you being available when a more suitable partner comes along.

Truth be told, I waited about a year after writing this book before I tried to get a publisher for it. Why? Because in that year I had taken a second job, which filled up all the time I had previously dedicated to the book. I also put off starting a podcast for that same amount of time, and for the same reason. Eventually, I had to come to terms with the fact that the second job wasn't getting me any closer to what I really wanted in a career, which is to spend my time evangelizing strategic quitting. What it *was* doing was preventing me from the opportunity to work on my passion. At the point I realized that the opportunity costs were outweighing the benefits of the second job, I made the quit.

As I mentioned earlier, it's normal to have a number of fears about quitting—some of which are likely productive fears and some less so. However, the one thing you *should* be afraid of is missing out on the chance to move on to something better. So don't miss out anymore—quit anything that's preventing you from being able to grab every last opportunity life sends your way!

Chapter 6

Is Time or Money Really Ever Wasted?

We already talked about the fallacy of sunk costs, and how no amount of time or money or effort already spent should have any effect on what you do with your future time, money, and effort. You may be completely on board with that and you're down with the quit, but there may still be a nagging feeling that time or money was 'wasted.' I put it in quotes because I'd like to examine what we mean when we say that word.

If you go to a coffee shop, buy a latte, walk outside, trip on an uneven sidewalk, and spill the entire thing before you even take a sip, then yes, technically the money you spent on that latte was wasted. You made an investment with zero return. But let's look at it another way. Maybe you walked into the shop, and your hands were freezing (this is where my California readers are just going to have to imagine what that feels like, but the rest of the country understands). You grab the latte, which is hot, and it warms up your hands. Now if drinking that latte was your ultimate goal, then true, your goal was not achieved. But you did gain both warmer hands and a knowledge of where in the sidewalk to avoid next time. However minor it may have been, you got something out of that venture.

While that may all be a stretch, it's the mental exercise that's important. If I can find two ways in which a five-minute trip to the coffee shop and a four-dollar investment on a coffee you never drank can lead to positive benefits, you can surely find the same in an academic endeavor or career pursuit that you wish you quit.

An example that's close to my heart is law school, which is an investment of at least three years and often hundreds of thousands of dollars. But the legal field is not for everyone, as the hours are demanding and the climate is often cut-throat. Thus it is not uncommon for me to hear from lawyers who desire to quit the field. Was their time and money spent on law school a waste if they quit? Absolutely not.

In law school you learn how to read and write contracts. And whether or not you realize it, you enter into multiple contracts daily, like when you bought that latte and your signature authorized the transaction, or when you downloaded the newest version of iTunes and chose to accept to their terms and conditions. The list is endless. So how useful is it to have learned how to read and interpret contracts? Very. Especially when the contract is no longer for iTunes, but instead is for buying a house or leasing a car. You learn so much in law school that's applicable to everyday life, even if it's just how to win an argument or to know when to yell 'Objection!' when watching courtroom dramas on TV.

The same applies to almost any pursuit. From a relationship that doesn't work out long-term, you learn what you do and do not want in your next partner. The same goes for a job you don't love. You not only learned whatever skills you were using in that job, but you also have a better idea of what you do and do not want in your next position.

A very thoughtful friend of mine was in attendance at a talk I gave recently on how to overcome the most common mental blocks that keep people from quitting. Afterward she said she understood everything I discussed about the sunk cost fallacy and how nothing was ever really a waste. She then said, "I know all of that intellectually, but we're all human, and I think we all still have those moments where we look back and regret having spent any time or money whatsoever on something that was wrong for us. How do you overcome that?"

I was thrilled she asked that question, because she's absolutely right. I can tell you everything that was covered in the last two chapters, and the rational parts of your brain can completely understand every word, but we're all human, and regret can rear its ugly head in even the most well-trained minds. Since she asked what I do in those circumstances, and I'll tell you what I told her. I've taken mental stock of my life and looked at all of the things I quit after dedicating some amount of resources to them; be it time, money, or even mental energy. When I take the retroactive long view of my experiences as a whole, I realize that each one of the endeavors that I later quit set me up in some way for something better, even if it wasn't immediately apparent at the time I quit, or even five or ten years later.

My first big quit illustrates this perfectly. I worked in multimedia from age 19-21, a career that would seem to be fairly useless in my later chosen fields of medicine and law. And true, for a good 15 years my multimedia skills lay dormant. But then I started a consulting company and needed a website, which I built myself, thanks to the graphic and web design skills I developed back when I worked in multimedia. Then I was hired at a digital media company where I had to do some minor graphics and web design. Again, these are skills I wouldn't have if I had gone the traditional path to medical school rather than having made a 180-degree career turn from multimedia.

Many describe this phenomenon using the phrase 'everything happens for a reason,' which I fully realize is truly insulting when you think about childhood cancer and genocide and other atrocities. Therefore, let me rephrase it a bit. Most things in my life have happened for a reason. Because on the whole, the concept does seem to have been overwhelmingly true in my particular journey.

When I look back at something that would typically lead me to feelings of regret, like "why did I ever get into that relationship?" or "why didn't I realize that I wasn't going to love medicine earlier?" I stop and remind myself that most things have happened for a reason, so whatever thing I'm lamenting at the time probably either has or will at some point play an important role in getting me to where I'm supposed to be.

Let me hippie out on you for just a minute. You may have heard the phrase "You're exactly where you're supposed to be." It's a favorite of the patchouli-sporting hemp-wearers of the world. But that doesn't make it less true, or more importantly, less comforting. It's essentially the present moment version of 'everything happens for a reason.' And as a non-religious person myself, who is still a human with a brain chock-full of the negativity bias that plagues most of our brains, I still sometimes need a slightly existential means of reassuring myself. Knowing I'm exactly where I'm supposed to be now (and therefore was exactly where I was supposed to be in all of those situations I later quit), is comforting and lets my brain stop riding the worry train and allows me to direct my thoughts in more productive directions.

To recap, I recommend you join me in reframing the idea behind 'wasting' time or money. Look back at the pursuit you are thinking of quitting and see all the knowledge and experience you gained from it. Then move forward, using that knowledge as your power. And if you end up looking back and start teetering toward regret, remind yourself both of that knowledge and of the fact that the universe tends to have your back, and whether or not you can see it now, there is probably a reason you expended those resources. Nothing wasted.

Chapter 7

Is Quitting Bad?

It's time to tackle one of the more sensitive topics in regard to quitting—whether or not quitting is 'bad.' I don't have to tell you how much moral weight people put on quitting. "Ahh don't be a quitter!" you hear. "Quitters never win!" There are so many blanket statement clichés encouraging people not to quit and to never give up that it would be hard to imagine that there isn't something almost immoral about quitting.

But is there? Let me separate the issue into two arenas: quitting as an act, in general, and quitting the specific pursuit you may be considering. First, let's tackle the latter: perhaps you are considering quitting a job where people rely on you. Perhaps your quitting will lead to others being laid off. Maybe you're the head of a start-up and if you quit, then investors will pull out and the entire company will fail. Those are really tough decisions, because they pit your best interest against the potential best interest of others. I myself was put in such a situation when I chose to quit a startup where I was the co-founder. The stresses of startup life had taken their toll on my health and led to increasing anxiety and intractable insomnia. I knew I had to leave, but I also knew that my quitting would both put huge additional burdens on my team, and it might have scared away potential investors. It was a decision I did not take lightly. I evaluated it through a lens you might find helpful in similar situations. If you are in a position where you're thinking of quitting, it's probably because the position has started to affect your mental or physical health in some way, as it had for me, which may be affecting your performance at work. Or even on a less severe level, your lack of desire to be at your job may be affecting, if only subconsciously, how much effort you put into it.

At that point, a new moral question arises: is it fair to your company for you to stay when you're performing at less than your best? See how that turns things around? You may have been so worried about what negative effect your leaving might have, when the effect of you staying may be just as negative. Remember that opportunity costs apply to your company as well. By having someone in a position where he or she doesn't fully want to be, the company is missing out on having another employee who may dedicate much more effort to the job.

The same concept applies even if it's not a job you wish to quit, but a marriage where children are involved. When you're considering the negative effects divorce may bring to the family, I suggest you also consider the effects on children of being raised in a home where there is constant fighting or tension between the parents. You may find there are moral arguments in favor of quitting in that situation as well.

Now that we've tackled the moral implications of specific quitting, it should be easier to answer the question of whether quitting, in and of itself, is a morally 'bad' behavior. It is absolutely not. There is nothing inherently bad about deciding any one course of action is not serving you and choosing to change course. Nada. Zilcho. In fact, I'd argue that the global community as a whole benefits when the greatest number of people are living their happiest lives. Happy people are less likely to engage in road rage or commit violent acts, and they generally make the world a kinder place. Therefore if quitting your job will make you a more pleasant member of society, then perhaps it's immoral *not* to quit.

Chapter 8

What Will People Think If I Quit?

Regardless of whether quitting is good or bad, you may be concerned about public perception of your choice to quit. And by public, I mean your friends, family, co-workers, and all foreseeable social media trolls.

Within humankind, there's a highly-evolved class of people who have the ability to put zero importance on what others think, no matter who that person is. On the other end of the spectrum there is another group with that same ability that psychiatrists have labeled 'sociopaths.' But if you're a mere average human like me, who occasionally considers what other people think, this should address your concerns.

People can react to any situation in one of three general ways: positively, negatively, or neutrally. The same goes for your quitting: some may be very proud of you, some may be disappointed or shocked, and some may not care at all. However, in all reality, most won't think about it in any of those ways for more than a minute. Imagine if right now you heard some news about a friend, and that news doesn't directly impact your life. You'd likely have an initial reaction, and then you'd probably go about your day. What you think about their situation likely has no effect on them.

Conversely, what they may think about your quitting, or anything else, will likely have no impact on you. So why stay in a job or relationship that makes you unhappy on the off chance that someone will think poorly of you? Unless that person is your spouse or boss or someone who could have a very direct impact on you, their judgments simply do not matter.

Once someone from a middle-eastern country told me his relationship with his wife was not working, but that they couldn't divorce because that wasn't allowed. I was curious. "It's illegal to divorce in your country?" I asked.

"No," he replied, "but the community would think poorly of me."

Since it pains me to see people making life decisions based on fear, I asked one more follow-up question. "What do those poor thoughts do to you? Aside from having to tolerate a side glance or two, do they negatively affect you in any real way?" And of course, the answer was no. It will almost always be no.

Recall that podcast with the 57-year-old psychiatrist who was quitting? She said her boss, and many others, thought she was crazy. The host pointed out, very astutely, that one man's crazy is another man's bold—that they're pretty much two sides of the same phenomenon and the label you choose is entirely dependent on your own frame of mind. The person who sees you quitting a well-paying but unfulfilling job, who has fallen into the 'comfortably numb' rut in his or her own job, will likely consider your choice crazy (if they consider it at all), but the people who have also made hard choices in order to further their careers and achieve their goals will likely view it as a bold and admirable step.

Regardless of how others view it, their thoughts are highly unlikely to have any adverse effect on you. However, the hard truth is that sometimes how a person views your decision to better your situation tells you all you need to know about whether that person is one who should be allowed into your inner circle. Surround yourself only with those who can contribute positive energy to your journey; who will support your dreams and encourage you to follow them, no matter how crazy they may seem to the nay-sayers.

In summary, if the worrying about what others may think of your quitting has kept you in a situation, I urge you to stop living out of fear and to start focusing only on what *you* think about your quitting. Because that thing you fear is fleeting, and if you give it no weight, it often has none. As a Navy Seal instructor once said on an episode of the *Freakonomics* podcast, "There is only shame in quitting if you feel it." I second that sentiment. Choose to quit shamelessly and choose to live joyously.

Chapter 9

Do Quitters Really Never Win?

It's time we address my least favorite saying: "A quitter never wins, and a winner never quits." Who said this anyway? Well, it was originally said by author Napoleon Hill in his book *Think and Grow Rich*. The book was about how to succeed in business. And while it may have been effective in the context of the book, its current widespread use, out of context, often does significantly more harm than good.

First, it's non-specific in regard to quitting. I'd argue that anyone who can quit smoking is a winner. Quitting a sugar habit is also a win. But let's assume for argument's sake that he meant quitting something other than an addictive habit. At that point it's still flawed because it uses an absolute term; never. It's common knowledge that one should question the validity of any statements containing absolutes. Even smoking, a habit that one should arguably 'never' start, is of some benefit to people with certain intestinal conditions. But my biggest argument is that it doesn't define what a winner is. Are you a 'winner' if you stay at a miserable job longer than anyone else? Are you a 'winner' if you stay in terrible relationships or investments long after they have proven themselves to be harmful to you? That doesn't sound like winning to me.

The second issue I have with the phrase is that it's just plain inaccurate in 99.9% of circumstances. To be fair, let's start with the only circumstance in which it *is* accurate;

sports. If you quit the Boston Marathon halfway, you will not win the Boston Marathon. No winner of an Ironman triathlon ever quit the triathlon they won. But even then, the applicability is so narrow, because there are plenty of people who have won races and other sporting challenges after having previously quit those same competitions. Quitting a 10k one year doesn't mean you won't win it the next year.

This phenomenon occurs in the world of professional sports all the time. Floyd Mayweather quit boxing in 2007 only to return in 2009 to fight, and *win*, against Juan Manuel Marquez. Randall Cunningham of the Minnesota Vikings football team had the best season of his career after coming out of retirement. And, arguably most famously, basketball great Michael Jordan retired from the sport in 1993 and switched to baseball, which he later quit and then returned to basketball. After those two quits, Jordan went on to win the NBA Finals with the Chicago Bulls three more times, during which he himself won MVP of both the regular season and All-Star Games.

Jordan quit multiple times. And Jordan won, multiple more times, after quitting.

In contrast to its occasional applicability in sports, the phrase 'quitters never win' is darn near 0% applicable in the business world. How many people do you know still work for the same company they worked for in high school? I'm going to guess very few. But how many of those same people would you consider successes? Probably a lot higher percentage.

This gets back to what I was saying in the first chapter— that it's all in how you look at a situation. Prior to medical school I worked in a lab reading electrocardiograms for cardiac-related academic studies. Then I got into medical school, which is a little bit like winning the lottery, because only something like one in three applicants gets in (ok, so better odds than winning the lottery, but almost as random, because many a person smarter than me has been rejected...I myself was rejected from 29 out of the 30 schools to which I applied. But I digress...). When it came time to start medical school, which is a full-time endeavor, I had to quit my job at the lab.

Does this mean I'm a quitter? Yes, according to our semantic discussion above. But has almost every single successful person had to quit one job to move up to another position or company or career? Also yes!

Quitting winners (or winning quitters) are everywhere. Let's start with one of the richest men in the world; Bill Gates. The man behind Microsoft (and curing polio around the world) is famous for having left (i.e. quit) Harvard after two years. Whether you measure winning in terms of financial success or worldwide impact, Gates is a clear winner, as his net worth is in the billions and his philanthropy through the Gates Foundation has touched millions of lives. So there, example #1 of quitter = winner.

Would you like another? Good! How about another Harvard dropout? Great! We've got Mark Zuckerberg, founder of Facebook and a philanthropic zillionaire. You want someone who actually graduated from Harvard and *then* quit? Look no further than author and filmmaker Michael Crichton of Jurassic Park and Westworld. He got his medical degree from Harvard Medical School, then quit medicine to become a writer.

Were they quitters? Yep—every single one. Winners? Undeniably.

For more on the 'quitters DO win' discussion, I'd love to give a huge shout out to Seth Godin, who wrote a book about quitting called *The Dip*. I highly recommend checking it out, because it's very short and almost every word is gold. But let me give you some of the Cliffs Notes on what he says in regard to winners and quitting. He said, "Winners quit fast, quit often, and quit without guilt." He also said, "Winners understand that taking [the short-term pain associated with quitting] now prevents a lot more pain later."

Finally, my favorite quote from the book, and maybe of all time, is "Winners quit all the time. They just quit the right stuff at the right time."

Chapter 10

What's the Difference Between Quitting and Failing?

I think a large part of the stigma around quitting is that it's confused for failure. Failure is defined as a lack of success. Therefore, to decide if one has failed, they must first define what success would have looked like for them.

Imagine that your definition of success in the career arena is getting into upper management at your company. You're currently in middle management, and you have been working for years in hopes of advancing, but to no avail. One day you decide to quit and change careers, and you end up doing something you really enjoy. Did you 'fail' because you didn't make upper management? If you are going strictly by your original definition, then yes.

However, I would argue that most of us define success slightly more abstractly—perhaps making enough money to support your family or finding a job where you enjoy going to work every day. If you quit your job without ever making it to upper management, but your new job is one you love that is still able to support you financially, that sounds like success to me.

Another distinction between quitting and failing is where the power lies. If you take a class you don't enjoy, and you do poorly in that class, the teacher may fail you. I've been there. I recall signing up for tap dance classes in college. I had taken tap dance lessons for years and thought it would be great to get class credit for it. However, the class was populated with semi-professional dancers who swept the floor with me. I realized instantly that if this class were graded on a curve, I would fail. So I quit on day one.

This illustrates my point that quitting gives YOU the power. I didn't wait around, powerless, for someone to tell me I'd failed. I saw a chance to cut my losses and switch to a class where I would fare much better. I took control. The power never left my hands.

Now, there is one similarity between quitting and failing. They're both often necessary steps along the path to success. Rarely does someone start a course in life and end up as a huge success, on that same path, with zero deviations. It's much more common that life takes twists and turns, with many successes and failures along the way. And quite often, changing course to redirect toward success requires quitting.

So join me in redefining success according to what would lead to your best life. Quitting is not failing. And even failing isn't fatal. They're both bound to be parts of a life where you take chances and put yourself out there. But if you find yourself in a situation that's not serving you, why not take the power back...and quit on your terms.

Chapter 11

Contemplating a Quit

Happiness is a journey, not a destination. For a long time it seemed to me that life was about to being - real life. But there was always some obstacle in the way, something to be gotten through first, some unfinished business time still to be serviced, a debt to be paid. At last it dawned on me that these obstacles were my life. This perspective has helped me to see there is no way to happiness. Happiness is the way. So treasure every moment you have and remember that time waits for no one.
- Alfred D. Souza

For years I had a magnet with this quote on my refrigerator because my life up to that point had seemed like a series of challenges to get through before I could be happy. Happiness was the proverbial light at the end of the tunnel, but the tunnel kept getting longer. First, I thought I'd be happy once I got into medical school, then it was once I finished medical school, then once I finished residency, and finally once I finished my fellowship. If you do the math, that's a total of nearly a decade I was waiting to be happy.

And was I magically happy after I finished all of those things? Sadly, no.

Are you in a similar situation? Are you in a tunnel with a light at the end? Or are you maybe in a tunnel with no light at all? Both of these are situations in which you may, and I would argue you should, contemplate quitting.

Let's examine the first possibility–that there is a light at the end of your tunnel. How long is that tunnel? How dark is that tunnel? The answers to those two questions are crucial to informing your decision about whether to quit. If you have one more semester of grad school and you find it hard but it's not soul-sucking, then it's probably in your best interest to stick it out and graduate. However, if you're in the sixth month of a seven-year neurosurgery residency and you're miserable, that's a whole different story.

Seven miserable years. Think of a bad day you've had. Then imagine the potential of 2,555 of those days in a row. Also, if you're miserable in your neurosurgery training, are you sure that the 'light' at the end of the tunnel is so bright? Is it the residency schedule you find painful, or the actual profession of being a surgeon?

There's a reason I bring up that specific example. At some point I was in residency. Granted, I was in a family medicine residency, which is nowhere near as grueling as neurosurgery, but still the concept is similar. My plan prior to medical school was to graduate with my medical degree, then do a family medicine residency, and follow that with a sports medicine fellowship. The light at the end of this tunnel was my dream job–becoming a sports medicine physician.

It was a very long, very dark tunnel.

While I was in medical school, many of my classmates said they had a hard time deciding what specialty to choose because they liked them all. This was shocking to me, because I didn't like any of them. I had decided that sports medicine was the holy grail of physician options because it didn't seem very medical at all (more often than not you're prescribing rest and ice) and because sports med docs are most often working with healthy, athletic people who take care of themselves. What I didn't stop to realize was that it also had a lot in common with the other fields of medicine that I found unbearable.

During medical school I wasn't energized by the work—it was a struggle to memorize the anatomy and all of the medications and conditions, but the even bigger struggle for me was that I didn't enjoy patient care. However, I persisted under the illusion that when I got through school, and then through residency, and finally into sports medicine, I'd be happy. As I said, with pre-med coursework included, that was a ten-year tunnel. I put my head down and forged through the tunnel, never stopping to examine what made me dislike patient care, or more importantly, whether what I disliked about patient care was going to be present in sports medicine. I convinced myself that sports medicine was the light at the end of the tunnel and that no matter how long or dark that tunnel was, the struggle would be worth it.

Let me deviate from the story here to ask you if you have been in this situation. Have you ever been so sure that light at the end of the tunnel was worth the pain, even though there may have been signs that it wasn't the panacea of awesome that you imagined it to be?

Let me tell you how my story turned out...after four years of medical school, I entered a residency in family medicine. It was three years of pure torture. Every third night I was on-call in the hospital for 30 hours straight. I had no life outside of the hospital, and sleep and exercise were nonexistent. Somewhere in that three-year period I started to notice something else—dealing with patients made my heart race. I was angry and negative. The glass was always half empty. My stress level was through the roof.

I can't imagine the damaging effect that 'surviving' for that long had on me. I'll delve thoroughly into the health benefits of quitting situations like this in a later chapter, but for now, just know that long-term stress is no bueno for your health.

What finally happened when I made it through the tunnel and got to sports medicine? I found out it truly was a dream job...sadly, it wasn't *my* dream. Turns out, to enjoy sports medicine, you should probably enjoy sports. I do not. Standing on the sidelines of sports I didn't understand, for hours upon hours, often at night or on the weekends, was the opposite of fun for me.

Let's review. I had struggled for ten years to get to the light, only to find darkness.

So what did I do after graduating from fellowship? I quit sports medicine. Having spent ten years to get to that point mattered not when the dream job was a nightmare. But instead of seeing all that time I spent as some kind of ball and chain that would keep me tethered to a career I didn't enjoy, I chose instead to see the reverse. I had put in too many years of extremely hard work to be miserable. And I highly recommend that if you find yourself in a similar situation, you tell yourself the same thing. All that work you fear will be 'wasted' was work you did to try to achieve a career or relationship that you love, and you are throwing it away by settling for something you don't.

If you happen to be trudging through a tunnel to get to the light, I offer some more insight from *The Dip*. Godin said, "Persistent people are able to visualize the idea of light at the end of the tunnel when others can't see it. At the same time, the smartest people are realistic about not imagining light when there isn't any."

Evaluate your tunnel. Evaluate whether that light is truly the beacon of awesomeness that you have made it out to be. Listen to your intuition. And if it tells you that this path isn't serving you, I invite you to consider quitting. And don't worry, the rest of the chapters will show you how it's done.

Chapter 12

What Specifically Should I Quit?

I hope the last chapter got you examining some different areas in your life where you may benefit from a quit. But as you examined those areas of your life, you also may have thought, "Eeek, a quit sounds really drastic…"

Let me allay your fears…quits do NOT have to be extreme. Sometimes the simplest quits can make a huge difference.

For a successful strategic quit, it's important that you quit the right thing, and only the right thing, which requires figuring out the specific area that isn't serving you. Because quitting ain't easy, the goal here is to get the maximum amount of benefit with the least amount of effort.

What do I mean by this? Imagine you are on a certain diet that requires you do extensive food preparation every week. You're seeing results on that diet. Maybe your health is improving, or your waistline is shrinking, but the thought of doing one more day of food prep fills you with dread. On a personal note, the thought of doing any cooking fills me with dread, so if you identify with this story, you're not alone. Anyway, is it the diet you should quit? No, it's the meal prep. If you have the means, there are food delivery services that provide pre-made meals according to most diets, so you can continue to reap the health benefits without having to spend what may be one of only two weekend days off slaving over the stove.

Now let's apply this to your job. If that's the thing that's making your stress level rise and your happiness level plummet, you may want to quit. But this is where specifics are important. Is it your specific position that you dislike? Is it instead the company culture, or perhaps your boss or coworkers? If your position in the company isn't working for you, but you love the company, then focus on quitting your position and trying to find another one within the same company that better suits you. Or perhaps don't quit the position, but quit an aspect of the job that you dislike by finding a better means of accomplishing the same task.

I did the same evaluation in my current job at the Veterans Administration, leading to a quit that may seem humorously insignificant to you, but I bet if you try hard enough you can think of an equivalently trivial-seeming quit that would make an equally big difference in your world. The bane of my existence used to be that the clinic where I work had fewer vital signs machines (the ones that take your blood pressure and heart rate) than there were doctors. This meant that if I wasn't the first one at work that day, my chances diminished of having access to one, and I have to take so many blood pressures a day (for the type of exams I do, I often have to take three blood pressures per patient), that having to do it manually would require at least an additional hour of work.

Why didn't they just buy more machines? Because I work for the government. I think the President himself would have had to have approved it.

This situation was subpar at best, infuriating at worst. There were plenty of things about my job that I didn't like, but nothing seemed so cruel as the fact that to avoid being there more hours (staying late due to extra time manually taking vital signs), I'd have to be there more hours (by getting in early to get a machine). Then one day I stopped by a colleague's office and saw she had bought her own vital signs machine. Whaaaa??? Yeah, because obviously Amazon sells those. Why hadn't I thought of that? Regardless, that's the day I quit letting the scarcity of machines make my job more frustrating than necessary and I bought my own machine.

Is that the tiniest quit? Probably pretty close to it. But has it made a huge difference? Indeed it has.

Remember the movie *Office Space*? Imagine if those guys could have quit printing things from the ill-fated printer, or if they could have quit putting cover pages on their TPS reports. Maybe they wouldn't have been quite so miserable.

Another quit that made a big difference in my life is slightly more esoteric, but no less impactful. I used to stress out about food 24/7. I would try to find out as much information as I could about different ways of eating, alter my diet daily based on the info I learned, and then try to make the foods I thought I was supposed to be eating, despite how much I looooathe cooking. If you had asked what the biggest stress in my life was at that time, it would have been keeping myself fed.

This may sound ridiculous to many. Most people who don't like to cook just get takeout. However, takeout didn't fit into my desire to be healthy, so I stressed…and stressed…

And then I quit. Not eating, obviously. I quit stressing about food. I quit researching information, and I quit trying to cook. I let a nutrition expert make a diet for me, and I found a food delivery service to bring me two meals a day…for about the same cost as I was paying for groceries. I no longer had to worry about what to eat and how to get the ingredients and whether I'd burn the kitchen down trying to cook them.

See how big a change a small quit can make?

Here's the last one from my quitting files. I used to have a membership to a yoga studio. The membership was only more financially advantageous than a ten-class pass if you made it to the studio twice a week. As a trained yoga instructor, I'm well aware I should be doing yoga at least twice a week, so I went with the membership. However, on the weeks I couldn't make it to class twice, I was losing money, and there were many weeks I wasn't making it that often. At that point I would stress about trying to get to yoga to make my membership worth the money.

Do you hear how counterproductive that sounds – stressing about yoga? Luckily, I also noticed how ridiculous that was, and I quit the yoga membership.

As I said before, these small quits are important because the thought of quitting your job may be overwhelming at this point. But if it's not your position that's causing issues, just a specific aspect of your job (like part of your workflow, or your commute), then those are much easier quits to make.

Imagine you love your job but hate the driving to and from every day. Just picture yourself doing the same job, sans commute, from the comfort of your home. How do you feel? Lighter? Then maybe it's time to quit commuting and ask the management if you can work from home.

Now if it's your relationship that's causing you stress, examine whether the stress is coming from the relationship itself, or just one aspect of the relationship. Perhaps the stress is that you two argue about who is going to clean the house. Well how about instead of quitting the relationship, you quit cleaning the house! Hire a housecleaner! Yes, it will cost a little, but if something so easy could take the stress out of your relationship, it may be a wise investment.

Here is your chance. Take a look at what concerns you and try to narrow down the specific aspects that aren't working. Those are the areas you should begin to examine as you contemplate a quit. And in the next chapter, we'll discuss how to finally decide if those aspects should stay or go.

Chapter 13

Deciding Whether to Quit

You've narrowed down exactly what parts of your life are keeping you from a more peaceful and fulfilling existence. Now, let's get down to making the actual decision; whether or not you should quit.

The first question to ask yourself is whether the things you dislike are fixable. This is akin to some of those small quits we discussed in the last session. Quitting something can be a form of fixing it. Like your commute, for example. If driving to work is your stress, can you fix it by taking public transport or asking to work from home? If you can fix what you dislike about something, there's probably no need to quit it entirely.

However, if you live an hour away from work, your boss won't let you work from home, and there are no public transportation options, that's an entirely different situation. This is where a quit may serve you well. If you can't fix your commute, it may be in your best interest to quit your job and look for another.

Take the relationship example from the last chapter. If fights over keeping the house clean are what brings you stress in your relationship, that's probably a fixable situation. However, if the tension in your relationship is due to one person's refusal to compromise or the fact that one person wants children and the other doesn't, that's probably not fixable. This is where it may be necessary to end the relationship.

Now the next step is crucial. If you have decided that the stressors are fixable, then envision fixing the aspects you dislike and staying in whatever situation had previously been stressful. How do you feel? Are you relieved to be able to stay? Are you happier in that situation? Or are you feeling more melancholy—like you were glad that a stressful part is gone but you still feel unhappy?

This is where your intuition steps back in as your biggest ally. You can't trick your gut feelings. You can't rationalize your way out of them. Your gut is only concerned with your best interest, so if it's still sounding the alarm after you've fixed whatever you thought may have been salvageable, it may be that a quit is in order.

Recall that startup I had to quit due to the effects it had on my health? Part of the stress was that we had yet to make any money, and I had been working for a year without any income from it. Obviously I had expected to work without payment for some time, but after a year it was really starting to drain me both financially and emotionally. I informed the founder of the company that I wanted to quit. He countered with an offer to begin paying me hourly for my work. So here, technically, was a 'fix' for one of the stressful aspects of the job–the lack of income.

However, when I imagined myself doing the same job under the same circumstances and only the payment was changed, I was still filled with dread. And that's all I needed to know. I turned down the offer and quit, and it was absolutely the best decision for me.

If you've arrived at the realization that your situation can't be fixed, but your intuition isn't giving you a strong enough sense of what to do, it's time to make a good ol' Pro and Con list. However, this one is slightly different. Start off listing the pros of staying and cons of staying, but also list the aspects of the thing you're contemplating quitting that you like and don't like.

I'll use the aforementioned yoga membership quit as an example of what this looks like.

Pros of the membership:
- I can go to unlimited yoga.
- I am more likely to go to yoga if I know I have pre-spent the money because I want the money to be worth it.

Cons of the membership:
- If I don't go to class often enough, I am wasting money.
- I stress about trying to fit in enough yoga classes per month to make the membership worth it. Sometimes I end up wasting the money because I can't go often enough.

Good aspects of the membership:
- Encouragement – I'm encouraged to go to classes I've already paid for.

Bad aspects of the membership:
- Lack of freedom – I feel trapped that I now have to go twice a week or I will lose money.

These aspects are really important, not just in decisions surrounding this quit, but in many future decisions. For example, this list helped me identify that memberships that depend on using a service a certain number of times cause me stress.

This type of list can also help you in identifying what you like, which should guide you in choosing your next endeavor. In fact, you may realize that the aspects that were good are easily found in another situation, which should help make the decision of whether to quit even easier.

While you're making lists, I also advise you make one more: a list of things you've already quit and the reasons you quit them. Check for patterns. Do you keep picking things with the same flaws? This is a great tool for making future decisions. Before taking another job or getting into another relationship, run down this list to make sure you're not getting into the same situation that hasn't previously worked.

So now that you have your list, do the pros outnumber the cons? Do the good aspects outweigh the bad? And how do you feel while having to list these? Paying attention to a combination of all three of those answers should be a great guide in letting you know if a quit is right for you.

Chapter 14

When Should I Quit?

If you're still reading, I'll assume you've decided you need to quit something. Congratulations! That's probably the hardest part. Truly, the rest is just details. But don't worry, I'm not going to leave you hanging—I'm here to help you through those details to make sure you have the most successful quit possible!

The timing of your quit depends on many factors, including what you're quitting and your personal circumstances. I can't cover every possible scenario, but I can go through a few categories into which most quits fall.

First up: quitting your job.

When is the right time to quit your job? Preferably before you have to, by which I mean, long before you're in danger of being let go, fired, or losing your mind. However, there are several additional aspects to take into consideration before bidding your job farewell, most of which are financial in nature. If you're independently wealthy or if your family is well-off enough that you don't need to work, then great, you can quit right away! Perhaps your only consideration would be making sure all loose ends are tied up so that you leave your superiors with a good impression of you, should you ever need a recommendation from them in the future.

However, for the rest of us, financial concerns are all too real, and are very often what keep people in undesirable jobs for years. NOTE: I am absolutely not advocating quitting with no plan in regard to your finances, especially if you have a family you are responsible for supporting, even partially. Maslow's hierarchy of needs will tell you that you can't be reaching your fullest self-actualized potential if you're worried about finding food and shelter.

Luckily, there are a few ways to quit your job and not send yourself into dire financial straits. One way to keep your finances afloat while you quit is to save money prior to quitting. Perhaps you plan your quit for a few months from now and in the meantime you make extra efforts to save up funds. Another way is to find a job you can do from home, on off hours, or part-time while you are in the process of finding another position. Whichever means you choose, be sure to do a thorough analysis of your finances, figure out how much you need to make per month to keep afloat, and don't quit until you're fairly certain you've found a way to come up with that amount.

Another of the considerations in when to quit your job is what you plan to do afterward. If you are looking to find a job working for someone else, which generally requires an application and an interview process, then your quitting timeline would differ from one whose goal is to start working for him or herself as a photographer or who plans to start writing a novel. You'll need to find a way to free up time during the day for interviewing, or find a part-time or work-from-home position that allows the same flexibility.

On the other hand, if you're going to start working for yourself or embark on a large project, you may want to start your project in the evening or weekend hours. These days more and more offices are letting their employees work from home, at least part-time. Therefore, it may be worth asking the management if you can switch up your schedule and work a few days a week from home.

Now what if none of the above options works for you? What if you're in a situation where you can't get any time off to interview for new positions? Then perhaps it's best to wait until you have some paid vacation time or some available sick days that you can use. And if you tell me, "No, there's absolutely no way I can get any time off during my current job to look for or interview at another employer," then you would probably be best served by saving up for a while to give yourself a couple of months of runway to allow you to find a new, more fulfilling (and clearly more flexible!) job.

While it varies by industry, it takes an average of 43 days to find a new job. However, that doesn't mean it takes 43 days to find the right job for *you*, just a job. So give yourself some extra time. You don't want to quit one unfulfilling job just to replace it with another. Find a creative way to support you and/or your family while finding a job that helps you live your best life.

Next up—quitting a relationship.

Similar to quitting a job, there are a number of factors that factor into the decision on when to quit a relationship. If you're single, you live separately from your significant other, and you have no children, then the decision on when to quit your relationship is probably pretty easy: as soon as you possibly can. No reason to hang on to something that isn't working for you if there are essentially no strings attached.

However, if you are married with children, the situation is totally different. I will be completely honest here—I have never been married and I have no children. The closest experience I have had to this is cohabitating with a significant other and aiming to keep our air plants alive.

Clearly dissolving a marriage involves legalities beyond the scope of this discussion. I highly recommend you seek legal advice and relationship counseling in regard to the specifics of a divorce. However, legal matters aside, the best solution is generally to start the proceedings as soon as possible.

Some of the few reasons that may warrant delaying a divorce include: waiting until the children have left home (if it's a short-ish period of time) and waiting until you have saved enough money to be self-sufficient. Otherwise, if you have already decided that ending your marriage is the right decision for you and your family, I would recommend doing it as soon as you can. Only then can healing begin and you can start to move toward your best life.

I realize that the bulk of you probably fall somewhere in between the no-strings relationship and married with children. In this case, you need to weigh the logistical factors involved in separating and being on your own. If you currently cohabitate with your partner, make sure you set yourself up financially to be able to live on your own. And if you are somehow otherwise connected through car or home leases or insurance matters, make sure to get those as in-order as possible prior to quitting.

Note that the caveat in all relationship quits is that if you are in an abusive situation, please ignore all of the above considerations and leave as soon as it is safe, contact the authorities, and, if necessary, find domestic violence assistance groups in your area.

Now as I said above, the list of possible quit types is long and I have only covered two. However, for all other quits, many of the same concepts can be applied: if there are financial or other strings attached, get those in order and then quit. If not, just quit. Which really just boils down to the following:

Quit as soon as it is logistically sensible.

Chapter 15

How Should I Quit?

Ok, whereas the 'when' of quitting was a fairly heavy topic, the 'how' is significantly easier. How should you quit? Kindly. Gently. In whatever way burns the fewest bridges. If you're in the middle of a big project at work that will be over in a few weeks, it would leave the best impression if you held out on quitting until the project ended. If your significant other has a major exam to take this weekend, maybe hold off on the breakup until after the test.

The gist is this: if a little courtesy on your part won't take too much of a toll on your sense of calm, then it's best to time your quit when it will be the least painful on the other party.

Now, you may be thinking that this is slightly out of line with the rest of my suggestions, as these quits are aimed toward improving *your* life, not others.' Often we avoid quitting because of the negative effects it may have on others, so enacting a quit forces us to put ourselves first for once. But how you quit can often have lasting effects on others that may later ricochet back to you.

Imagine you quit during the big project at work, or you leave your partner the day before his or her big exam—what kind of impression will that leave? Your current boss may well be the one who decides whether to write you a letter of recommendation for your next job. And your current partner can either become a civil friend or a lifelong enemy depending on the last impression that you left during the separation.

One more thing. When you do quit, do it with kindness. Again, there is no reason to write a nasty letter to your boss or have a big breakup brawl, as they both leave an unnecessarily bad impression.

That's about all there is to it. As promised, the 'how' of quitting is fairly straightforward. Quit as kindly and gently as possible. I promise it will pay dividends in the end.

Chapter 16

Preparing Your Health for a Quit

This chapter covers a topic very close to my heart. Mostly because it involves my heart. Literally. And your heart, too. Not the woo-woo 'heart' from greeting cards and love songs. The actual organ that delivers blood throughout the body.

We're going to prepare your health for a quit.

If you are quitting the right things for the right reasons, your health should benefit. Tremendously. Back in medical school I was in a relationship with someone who, almost amusingly in retrospect, disliked doctors. As you could imagine, my being on the road to doctorville was putting a strain on our relationship. A big strain. Around the same time, I started having heart palpitations. But since I was in class 12 hours a day—including on September 11, 2001— when I had to dissect a body in anatomy lab while the World Trade Center attacks were taking place, I assumed that if anything was giving me heart palpitations, it was school and/or terrorism.

It wasn't.

I went to the emergency room one night with palpitations, and they said there was nothing wrong with me physically. I wore a heart monitor for a day. Nope, no issues with my heart. A few days later my then-boyfriend and I got into an unusually heated argument. Suddenly I was struck with chest pain. Then I couldn't breathe. Then I fell to the floor.

I was having a panic attack.

Luckily, even though I was only a few months into medical school, I somehow knew this was a panic attack and not a heart attack. But that knowledge didn't take away the pain, nor the panic.

The next day I quit that relationship. I've never had a panic attack like that again.

This is a pretty extreme example of how your health can suffer when you stay in a situation that's not serving you. And how quitting can be quite beneficial for your health.

However, let's look at the flipside. Because while quitting is likely to lead to an improvement in your health, the quit itself isn't always a health-promoting endeavor, as it's often a time of stress and anxiety. Also, if you plan to work one job while trying to look for another, or while starting your own business, you may be putting in more work hours than usual. This will likely require extra energy. Therefore, a good pre-quit strategy is to get your health in the best shape possible prior to starting the transition.

Here are some very basic tips (consult with your physician for specifics based on your individual health):

1. Get your sleep schedule in order. Set a rough bedtime and stick to it. Do the same with your wake-up time. I go to sleep between 10:30-11:00 each night and wake up between roughly 7:00 and 8:00 every day, but that wasn't always the case. I used to have a really difficult time falling asleep each night and rarely got 6 hours of sleep until I adopted a sleep schedule. As you probably know, insufficient sleep can lead to fatigue, anger, anxiety, and weight gain… none of which is going to help during your quit.

2. Pay attention to your diet. Are you living off junk food? How's that working for your energy level? Or are you in my former situation, where you're so obsessed with finding the perfect foods that it's taking up way too much of your brainpower? Now would be a great time to simplify your diet while also making it as healthy as possible for your situation. Often this comes down to finding some general healthy guidelines and buying staples in bulk that you can easily make day after day.

As is the case with many aspects of life, the less energy you have to spend making trivial decisions, the better equipped you are to deal with the more important decisions. So while the decision of whether to have a chicken breast or a kale salad for lunch may seem trivial, when you have to eat at least three times a day, every day, the decisions add up. So why not apply Steve Jobs' wardrobe method to your meals? Pick something that you're going to eat for lunch every day that week, make five of them on Sunday, and then you're set for the week. You'll probably stretch your grocery budget further with that small amount of planning as well.

3. Start exercising. If you already exercise, you know how much it helps regulate your sleep cycle and increases endorphins (the feel-good chemicals in your brain). These and so many more reasons are why exercise is crucial during the lead-up to your quit. The time during a quit can be stressful, so the stress relief is a huge bonus, as is the burst of happiness that exercising can bring.

In addition, if you are out of shape, doing little things like walking up four flights of stairs to an interview could leave you winded when you finally meet your employer, something a little exercise ahead of time could prevent. Therefore, the pre-quit preparation phase is a great time to start making exercise a priority and working it into your schedule.

4. Take care of existing medical issues. Conditions such as a thyroid imbalance, high blood pressure, or diabetes can all affect your overall energy level and feeling of well-being. If you've been neglecting a medical condition, now would be a great time to get it under control so you can be in optimal shape to take on the challenge of reshaping your life.

Also, if you are planning to quit your job, or a marriage or domestic partnership, then your health insurance may become an issue. If your quit is likely to leave you without health insurance (at least temporarily), then I'd advise getting whatever yearly checkups you may need prior to leaving. And if you have a health issue that needs attention, make an appointment to be seen while you still have insurance.

Finally, there's the issue of mental health. As I discussed above, if you neglect your mental health, your physical health may suffer. Depression can leave you too fatigued to go about your regular job, so imagine how hard it would be if you left depression untreated and tried to add a second job during your transition. Similarly, anxiety is bad enough in normal daily activities, but if untreated, imagine how much more frightening your interviews could be. The quitting process is one of uncertainty, by nature, and there are likely to be a lot of ups and downs along the road. In order to deal with those ups and downs, it's important to have the best possible mental state in place.

If you have any concerns about mental health, I'd recommend talking to your doctor about seeing a therapist. And if you're concerned about the stigma (while dwindling, thankfully) about seeking help with your mental health, I offer this: You have two types of health; mental and physical. You go to a personal trainer to help you get your physical body in shape, so why would you not go to a therapist to get your mind in shape? Your mind affects everything else! This quit is about increasing your happiness, right? Where does happiness exist? Where all feelings originate: the mind. So please, there are about a million types of mental health assistance out there, from face-to-face therapy to therapy apps to meditation and yoga. Find one (or more than one) that works for you.

Since I'm a doctor I could go on about preparing your health all day. But I won't. Because I am not *your* doctor. I can give you some general recommendations, but I still highly recommend that you see your personal physician. What I'm essentially saying is, "Take two of these, but call someone else in the morning."

Chapter 17

Preparing Your Finances for a Quit

Finances are often a large concern while preparing for a quit, and they should be. As I mentioned before, the hierarchy of needs dictates that it's quite difficult to achieve a state of peaceful happiness when you are homeless and have no idea when you will eat next. So let's go over some basic ways to try to ensure that you're financially stable as you make your quit.

Clearly the finance situation is most crucial if the thing you plan to quit is the job that pays your bills. Let's then focus on that situation first—preparing to lose the main source of your income. There are a few ways to handle this. The most basic is to save money prior to quitting. However, that may not be feasible, especially if you're living paycheck to paycheck. If that's the case, you may be required to take a really hard look at your finances. Could you add a roommate? Move to a cheaper living situation or different area of town? Do you live in a city where selling your car is an option? Can you ditch the daily latte splurge? There are a number of ways to pare down your cost of living.

The real issue arises when you've done all of those things and are still barely making ends meet. Recall that as a last resource, there is always unemployment which may (depending on the circumstance of your quit) cover you for a few months. Note, this is more likely to be an option for you if you are let go or somehow get your job to release you. For example, in California, you can't receive unemployment if you are unemployed through any fault of your own, as determined by California law. So please, do not assume this is an easy backup option—I just wanted to mention it as I do know friends who have used it to help in their transition.

What if none of the above are options? Well here's another one from the cringe files—consider moving in with your parents. I know, depending on your relationship with your family, or their financial situation, this may not be desirable or even possible. But it's also nothing to be ashamed of if it's part of a plan to get you to a better situation where you can be financially stable and living your best life.

Now, since I'm far from a financial expert, I decided to reach out to my network for some additional tips for a financially savvy quit. I know two CPAs who quit the finance world and went into vastly different careers: one is an actor, and another is a professional beer brewer.

The actor said that his one tip for preparing your finances would be to adjust your thinking on which jobs you think are, for lack of a better term, beneath you, at least in terms of hourly pay. He pointed out that a $50,000 a year salaried job, which most would consider respectable, may not actually garner that much per hour after you consider taxes and any unpaid overtime that comes with a salaried position. That's something to keep in mind if you're in the transition period between jobs and are offered a position that seems menial or significantly beneath your pay grade. It may be worth it to take that job in the interest of keeping a positive cash flow in the short term.

The brewer offered me the advice he himself used when transitioning from finance to brewing. He downgraded enough to be able to live on half of his salary. This is clearly advice you need to start while you are still in the job you plan to quit, but it's also great advice for how to live once you've found your new gig. He said that once you're able to live on half your salary, then try living on a quarter of your salary. This accomplishes two goals: First, you will be able to save money for the time when you finally make the leap, but it also helps you identify areas where you could be saving money, which will be of great use should there be lean times during the transition. With his technique, if you come upon a month without any income, you'll have a reserve and won't suddenly have to sell your car or move immediately—you'll already have pared things down to only what's truly necessary.

There are non-work-related quits that may also affect your finances. Two that come to mind are quitting an educational pursuit and quitting a relationship. If you're in an expensive degree program, and you're not using loans to pay for it, quitting it may actually benefit you financially. However, if you are halfway through something you've taken out significant loans to pay for, like professional school (medicine, law, etc.), and you quit before graduation, paying back whatever loans you accrued during the portion of the program you did attend may be difficult without that final degree.

My brother experienced this very dilemma—he actually finished law school but decided not to take the bar or practice law, so he had to find a way to pay back a $160,000 loan without a high-paying law career. What did he do? Well first he tried substitute teaching and living with my parents while trying to find a job that paid well enough to cover his loan payments. In two years of trying, he never found that job. So he joined the Army…at age 30. No kidding. We thought he was crazy to do something that seemed so drastic to pay off his loans, but luckily for him, the Army was a great choice and he excelled in it and is very successful in his military career. But quitting law without a plan led to a very rough two years and a move to the military that not everyone would want to undertake, so let his be a tale of caution—make sure you really want to do law or medicine prior to accruing extreme debt.

However if you *are* halfway through an expensive degree am I telling you NOT to quit? By no means! But it would be irresponsible of me to ignore the reality of student debt. I have a quarter million dollars of it, and its presence shapes decisions I make every day. Despite my multiple quits, I have found ways to make my law and medicine degrees work for me in ways that make it possible to pay those loans, but in the lean, in-between job times, it wasn't easy. And sadly there aren't any easy answers to this conundrum.

This is where I'm going to get into the nitty gritty just a bit. If you are miserable in your degree program and know you would never want any job said degree would help you get—then quit before you accrue more student loan debt. But, if you are in a program and the degree will help you get jobs you may love, just not the exact job you imagined, I'd be less likely to suggest you give it up.

Take law school. With a law degree you can be a lawyer, but you can also go into politics, or business, or contract reviewing, or certain types of consulting. Therefore, if you're in law school and the thought of going the typical law firm route doesn't appeal to you, but one of those other routes does, then perhaps you should stick it out. However, if you're like my brother who decided he wanted nothing to do with anything that required a law degree, then perhaps getting out sooner rather than later would serve you well.

You may have noticed that nowhere in here do I present a great solution to how to deal with your student loans if you started accruing them and then choose to quit school without finishing. That's because I'm not sure anyone has a great solution to student loan debt—most of us are just saddled with it with no foreseeable way out. But there are several federal programs aimed at reducing debt or at least your monthly burden, like income-based repayment, so I'd check out studentaid.ed.gov to see what assistance may be available.

Next up: relationships. If you happen to be in one of those no-strings attached relationships I described in the chapter on when to quit, then you probably have little to do in the way of preparing your finances for a quit, as you are probably not intertwined financially with your partner. But if you are cohabiting or married, then money may be a significantly bigger concern.

If you are married and thinking of divorce, again, this is where I highly recommend you consult with a divorce lawyer before making any decisions. Each state differs on how finances and assets are divided after divorce, and each individual marital situation is unique, so it is beyond the scope of this book to advise on what may happen with your joint finances post-divorce.

However, there are two common scenarios of marriage dissolution I will address: the breadwinner and the home-engineer. By home-engineer, I am referring to the person who may not work outside of the home but who nevertheless works hard at either raising the children or keeping the household in order. Back in the day it would have been called a homemaker, but something feels very antiquated about that term, so I'm going to use a different one.

First - the breadwinner. This is the one who is paying most or all of the family's bills. Clearly, a split will be financially easier on breadwinners than those who don't currently have a source of income, but the breadwinner should be prepared for additional expenses such as child support or alimony payments. If those are likely to dig deeper into your pockets than you are prepared for, I'd suggest prepping for your quit by using one of the money saving techniques above.

Second - the home-engineer. A marital split will hit hardest if you have no current source of income. So if a divorce is in your future, I would highly advise consulting a financial professional (perhaps someone in your circle can provide you discounted services) ahead of time so that the split is less financially jarring. It may require finding your own home, car, and job all nearly simultaneously. I would highly advise availing yourself of whatever family and friend support you can, as it can help ease the transition. Also, try employing the strategies listed above to save money ahead of time, and look for creative ways to start drawing some income.

The home-engineer situation is significantly more severe if it's a cohabitation that's dissolving and not a marriage, as a divorce usually provides some spousal support, but a cohabitation does not. Know that you can do it—we are all stronger than we think, and we can make it through difficult situations. But also know that there is no shame in asking for help from friends, family, and your network. Those who love you will probably be happy to help you out of a less-than-ideal situation.

Chapter 18

Preparing Your Relationships for a Quit

Just to be clear, this chapter isn't about preparing to quit your relationships, it's about preparing your relationships for an upcoming quit. Because while quitting is likely to bring a long-term upward shift in your happiness level, it may be quite the opposite in the short-term.

Let's assume for the purposes of this discussion that you're quitting a job (and not a relationship, or this chapter would be moot!) Having to cut back on expenses, finding a new job, and giving your two weeks' notice to the management are all things that can bring stress, and stress can surely take its toll on relationships. It's crucial to make sure that your partner is aware of this ahead of time and is ready to help you through it.

First, if you and your partner are having any issues pre-quit, the stress of a quit can magnify them. Therefore, this would be a great time to address those issues, either between yourselves or with a couples' therapist. As I mentioned in the health chapter, there are so many types of therapy these days that if one type seems daunting, there are a number of other choices. I highly advise sorting out pre-existing relationship issues because your partner can either be your greatest support through your quit, or hugely detrimental.

Imagine you're exhausted from a day of interviews and you come home to a partner who's decided to make you dinner or give you a massage. Now imagine that same scenario, but instead you come home to an angry partner who immediately delves into a fight about finances or doing the dishes or whatever you had fought about a hundred times the day before. One of these two situations is going to re-energize you to keep up the fight, and another may break your resolve to quit altogether. I can't stress enough the importance of setting yourself up for the former.

The transition from one job to another may also lead to a significant change in the amount of time you spend with your significant other. If you quit and start working from home, or go through a period of unemployment, you may be around the house a lot more, and if you cohabitate or are married, this can mean more time spent together and less alone time for either of you. That's something to address. Perhaps if you or your partner need more alone time, find a way to conduct your job search from a coffee shop or co-working space.

Alternatively, if you are trying to start your own side gig while still working a 9 to 5 job, then you may be working most of the day and night. Your partner needs to be prepared for this and know to not take it personally if you can't spend as much time together as you had previously. However, this is not a one-sided endeavor—you can't just tell your partner to be understanding and hope it happens. It requires you knowing what you can do to keep him or her feeling loved and secure during this time of transition.

It also may call for a redistribution of tasks or chores, especially in marriage/cohabitation scenarios. If you always made dinner and your partner always did the finances, perhaps you could switch if you're no longer home at dinnertime and taking care of the finances now fits your schedule better. Or perhaps a housecleaner could come in handy so that one person isn't saddled with all of the chores while the other works two jobs.

There is a myriad of ways your relationship could change, and it requires effort on both of your parts to keep things working smoothly. If you have a loving partner, he or she will likely want to support you in any way possible. However, be mindful not to take advantage of this and let his or her needs go by the wayside. Do whatever you can to be as present and devoted to the relationship as you can by finding out what ways, no matter how small, you can show love and respect and dedication to your partner.

Chapter 19

Quitting an Identity

(The Hardest Quit)

Have you digested all of the above information, realized something isn't serving you, and yet you're still not ready to quit? If so, I have a good guess as to why: you've built an identity around the thing you're trying to quit.

If you're not familiar with what counts as an identity, you'll notice it usually falls after the phrase 'I am.' Here goes:

I am a father.

I am a dog owner.

I am an athlete.

I am an intellectual.

I am a wife.

I am a healer.

I am a football fan.

If I asked you to fill out a profile for yourself (like a dating profile, but one where you *weren't* trying to impress someone), what would it include? Here's mine: *I am a dancer. I am a musician. I am a rational, logical person. I am a doctor.* All of those things I say I am are huge parts of my identity.

Think of what those are for you. Maybe you're a skateboarder, an artist, a vegan, a hunter, or an activist. Now imagine having one of those taken away. Imagine you used to identify as an artist but you can no longer create art. What would that feel like?

Hopefully you now begin to see the issue—imagine that your identity is built around being a wife, yet your marriage is in shambles and the stress is taking its toll on your health. How much harder is it to walk away when doing so means that you may no longer know who you are?

I point this out not to say that it is by any means impossible to quit an identity. It is absolutely possible. Instead, I mention it to let you know that if you're to quit an identity, your road may be harder, and that you shouldn't be overly self-critical if the quit isn't going as easily as you may have imagined it would.

So how does one quit an identity? As with so many other processes, the first step is acknowledging that that's what you're trying to do. Not many of us have spent much conscious effort figuring out what our identities are. But let's take the time to try it now. Like I said above, imagine that you're filling out some kind of profile. Facebook, Twitter, and Instagram all have sections where you get to say whatever you want to about yourself. If you're on Twitter, scroll through a few profiles of those you follow and see what they say. You'll likely see a combination of the following categories: parental status (i.e. 'Mom of three'), job title, religious affiliation, and hobbies.

Lest you think this applies only to millennials, here are some of the Twitter bios of famous people who aren't millennials but whose self-descriptions are great examples of identities in action:

- LeVar Burton (of the Roots and Reading Rainbow fame): "Actor, Director, Educator, and Student."
- Leonardo DiCaprio: "Actor and one of the best Environmentalists."
- President Barack Obama: "Dad, husband, President, and citizen."

- Richard Branson: "Tie-loathing adventurer, philanthropist, and a troublemaker, who believes in turning ideas into reality. Otherwise known as Dr. Yes at @virgin!"

I'll even give you my Twitter bio. For my personal account, it says: Physician. Adjunct law professor. Election reform enthusiast. Capoeirista.

Delving into the above, I must first explain what a capoeirista is—it's someone who trains the Brazilian martial art of capoeira. I've done it for over seven years and it's a huge part of my identity. I can't imagine quitting capoeira, but realistically, one day I will probably have to make that decision. I don't know any 80-year-old women training capoeira, and while I would love to be the first, I'm aware that may not happen. I may move somewhere that doesn't have a capoeira group, or I could develop some other issue or injury that prevents training.

While quitting capoeira would be hard, it wouldn't be impossible, because as you saw in my Twitter profile, I have some backup identities. And you probably do too, which is crucial to remember if you're trying to quit something around which you've built an identity.

I have never been married, but I can imagine that being a spouse is a powerful identity. Someone has replaced your name with 'my wife,' 'my husband,' or 'my partner.' Now what happens if that relationship is something you feel is holding you back? How do you go from being 'wife' or 'husband,' back to just you? By remembering that before you were someone's spouse, you were someone. Who was that person? Were you a cook, a soccer player, a movie buff? You still probably are. Almost everyone has multiple talents or passions that would continue to exist even if one of them fell away.

As a side note, if you did this exercise and couldn't fill in the blank with anything, I'd urge you to ask your friends what they think of when they think of you, or how they would describe your passions. If that fails, examine your life more closely. What do you look forward to? Do you love a certain type of music, TV show, movie, dance, video game, or sport? Are there causes you believe in, like saving the environment or empowering the underserved? Do you have a talent for listening when your friends need a shoulder to cry on or are you a natural leader? These can all be identities. Heck, some people make identities out of being unlike anyone else (the mavericks, the rebels, the outsiders).

Much of the difficulty in quitting an identity comes from the fact that it requires reframing your thoughts about who you are at your core. In *You Are a Badass at Making Money*, Sincero hits the nail right on the head: "When you change who you're being, you're basically killing off your old identity, which completely freaks your subconscious self out."

You'll note she said 'subconscious' – and that gets back to what I said above, which is that you may not even realize that you have an identity, much less that it's built around the thing you need to quit. But that's why the above exercise is important—it helps you identify your primary and backup identities.

By the way, there's one more option for those fearing the loss of an identity: creation of a new one. You've likely heard countless stories about people who have created whole new lives for themselves after a quit. There's the stay-at-home mom who takes up yoga after the kids leave home, the former high-powered lawyers who become musicians, and of course, George W. Bush, who took up painting dogs once he was no long President (ok, so he didn't 'quit' being President, but it's just such an amusing post-career hobby choice and he's so public about it that I had to bring it up.).

This means you can look at your post-quit life as a blank slate if you choose. So you're not going to be a (fill in the blank) anymore…what do you want to be now? When the self-help gurus tell you to live your best life, there's nothing that says it has to bear any resemblance to your current life, so feel free to entirely reinvent yourself, complete with new passions and identities.

Chapter 20

Overcoming Fear

You made it to the last chapter, which means you're totally ready to quit, right?

Well, I hope so, but there may be one last thing standing in your way:

Fear.

Yeahhhhh…so if you haven't noticed, fear is probably standing in the way of a lot more than your quit. It's the same little monster that keeps you from approaching that person you find intriguing and attractive, from asking your boss for a raise, and from starting your own company. Fear is a total jerk and I simply can't imagine how different the world would look if it didn't loom so large in everyone's lives.

But it does. So what do we do? Let's be honest—if I had a cure-all for fear I'd be a ridiculously wealthy woman. But I can offer a list of suggestions on how to overcome it, alongside a boatload of encouragement to get you to believe that you are strong enough to attack that monster head-on and come out on top.

First I'm going to ask you to write down a list of your successes. These don't have to be huge wins—just think of anytime you accomplished anything difficult. Were you a hit in your junior high talent show? Did you score a competitive scholarship to college? Did you learn to juggle or ride a horse or win 'best orchid' in your neighborhood plant competition? Put it all on the list. Every last success.

Then get out a second piece of paper and write down what your new life looks like post-quit. Imagine your best-case scenario. Write it out in full detail, including how you feel in that new situation. Make it super detailed. No matter how ridiculous you may feel, it's much harder to achieve a goal you can't imagine, so start imaging it.

Now on one last piece of paper write down what scares you about quitting. If you can't quite put your finger on it that's probably a good sign—it means you just have the general fear of change that's ingrained in most of us. However, let me still give you some possible fears:

1. Fear of quitting one job and not finding another.
2. Fear of quitting a relationship and not finding another.
3. Fear of quitting an educational pursuit and later wishing you hadn't.
4. Fear that you won't be able to support yourself financially.
5. Fear that your entrepreneurial venture will not succeed.
6. Fear that your creative endeavor will be rejected by society.

As synchronicity would have it, just as I got to this point in writing this chapter, I heard a podcast that dealt with how to overcome fears in making big decisions. The podcast guest was Tim Ferriss, author of of *The Four Hour Workweek*.

Tim talked about dealing with fear in a few ways. First, he said he riggs the game so that he'll win even if he fails. For example, he said (in reference to starting a podcast) that if the podcast failed, at least he would have had the success of improving his interviewing skills and reaching out to people. He would ask himself before starting an endeavor, "How can I win even if this fails?" and then he would write out the answers.

He also talked about a chapter in his book *Tools of Titans* that covers a process he calls "fear-setting." He believes the first step to conquering fear is to define the fear, and to do that he recommends the following procedure. Take whatever decision is causing fear (like the decision whether to quit) and write down the worst-case scenarios that can happen (and let your imagination go wild—write out every last detail of the outcomes). Then evaluate whether those outcomes are likely to be or would truly be permanent, along with the impact on your life if they were, on a scale from 1 to 10 (10 being the most impactful). Next, write down what you can do to minimize the risk of those things happening, and finally, write down how you could get back to where you are now if the bad outcomes do occur. (Note: Tim Ferris's full 'fear-setting' procedure is seven steps long and significantly more in-depth than I have covered here, but I have limited it to the most high-yield steps, and I strongly recommend you check out his book for the full chapter if you have any lingering issues with fear).

Wanna see it in action? At some point I had to decide whether I was going to start coaching people on quitting and set up a website to help people quit and write this little book here. Was I afraid it would fail? Indubitably.

So I asked myself, "What's the worst that can happen?" To which the answer was, "No one finds your information useful, no one ever asks you to coach them or to give talks on quitting, and zero people buy your book."

The next question was, "What's the likelihood those occur and what permanent impact would it have on your life?" The sheer volume of people who are unhappy in their careers led me to believe that there had to be someone out there who would find my information beneficial, so being a 100% failure wasn't super likely. But even if I failed spectacularly, it would have had little to no permanent impact on my life. It would probably have been a short-term monetary setback due to the expense of setting up a website and publishing the book, but neither that nor the little ego hit

You made it to the end! That means you didn't QUIT the book, though I would have been just as excited if you had strategically quit reading it!

If you found the information in Quitting by Design valuable and would like to help more people find the book, I would greatly appreciate you leaving a review on **Amazon** (or buying one for a friend while you're there!)

And I'd love to see where you read the book. Post a photo and tag @quittingbydesign to share!

Together we can spread the message that quitters DO win!

Much love,
Lynn Marie

I would have taken would have left a lasting mark on my life.

I set up the website and wrote the book.

And even if you are the only person who reads this book, my worst fears have been averted. And I'm guessing you'll find whatever fears you may have will eventually be averted, too.

You ready to do this? To face your fears? To leave whatever isn't working for you behind? To stop settling?

Good, you deserve it.

And you *are* ready. You've got this.

Get out there and start quitting.